D. B. COOPER

BY ARNOLD RINGSTAD

Apex is distributed by North Star Editions:
sales@northstareditions.com | 888-417-0195

Produced for Apex by Red Line Editorial.

Photographs ©: Shutterstock Images, cover, 8–9, 10–11, 13, 14, 18 (left), 18 (right), 19, 24–25; iStockphoto, 1, 4–5, 6, 7, 21, 26–27, 29; AP Images, 16–17, 20; Eric Risberg/AP Images, 22–23

Library of Congress Control Number: 2022911080

ISBN
978-1-63738-432-9 (hardcover)
978-1-63738-459-6 (paperback)
978-1-63738-511-1 (ebook pdf)
978-1-63738-486-2 (hosted ebook)

Printed in the United States of America
Mankato, MN
012023

NOTE TO PARENTS AND EDUCATORS

Apex books are designed to build literacy skills in striving readers. Exciting, high-interest content attracts and holds readers' attention. The text is carefully leveled to allow students to achieve success quickly. Additional features, such as bolded glossary words for difficult terms, help build comprehension.

TABLE OF CONTENTS

CHAPTER 1

ESCAPE INTO THE NIGHT

It was November 24, 1971. A plane was flying from Portland, Oregon, to Seattle, Washington. A man bought a ticket. He used the name Dan Cooper.

In the 1970s, airports had less security than they do today.

After the plane took off, the man said he had a bomb. He demanded four parachutes and $200,000. When the plane landed, the passengers got off. The pilots stayed. Cooper told them to fly to Mexico City.

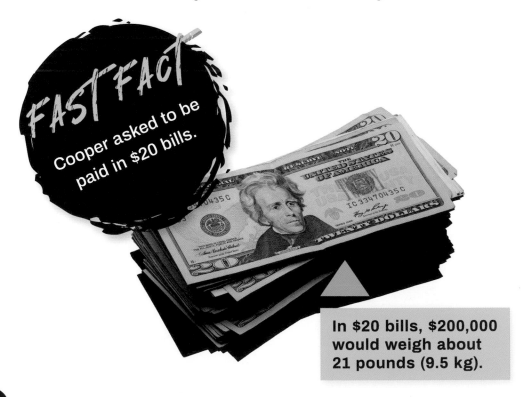

FAST FACT

Cooper asked to be paid in $20 bills.

In $20 bills, $200,000 would weigh about 21 pounds (9.5 kg).

Skydivers use parachutes to fall from the sky without getting hurt.

During the flight, Cooper jumped from the back of the plane. No one ever saw him again.

Boeing 727 airplanes were used by many different airlines.

PICKING A PLANE

Cooper chose a flight on a Boeing 727. This type of plane has a stairway that can lower from the back. A person can jump out safely.

CHAPTER 2

THE SEARCH BEGINS

The police learned that Dan Cooper was a fake name. A reporter called the hijacker D. B. Cooper by mistake. This wrong name caught on.

Police thought Cooper likely jumped from the plane near Ariel, Washington.

FBI **agents** got involved. The agents talked to many people. They tried to find out who Cooper was. Some thought he was a **skydiving** expert.

FAST FACT

The FBI called its investigation NORJAK. This meant "Northwest Hijacking."

FBI agents often team up with police officers to solve crimes.

Before being used, parachutes are folded up inside packs.

Cooper jumped with two parachutes. One was a training model. It was sewn shut. Police gave it to him by mistake. A skilled skydiver would have noticed.

FOUR PARACHUTES

Cooper didn't say why he wanted four parachutes. He may have wanted police to think he'd take someone with him. Then he'd be sure to get working parachutes.

CHAPTER 3

SUSPECTS

The FBI agents studied the case. They looked for evidence. They talked to the plane's crew. They had many suspects.

The plane's crew said Cooper was a tall, middle-aged white man wearing a suit.

One was Richard Floyd McCoy. He did a similar hijacking a few months later. Like Cooper, McCoy used a parachute. But he didn't match how the crew described Cooper.

Cooper claimed to have a bomb in his suitcase. McCoy used a hand grenade.

After a cigarette touches someone's mouth, it has that person's DNA on it.

MISSING EVIDENCE

Cooper left used cigarettes on the plane. These could have been used to test for his DNA. The FBI tried to send them to a lab. But they got lost on the way.

In 2011, Marla Cooper claimed the hijacker was her uncle. She said he lost the money while jumping. But the FBI didn't think it was him, either.

People used helicopters to search the area where Cooper might have landed.

The search for Cooper got people's attention. They made art based on him.

CHAPTER 4

CLOSING THE CASE

n 1980, a boy was playing along the Columbia River. He found a package containing $5,800. Police checked the bills. They matched the money given to Cooper.

When a boy found D. B. Cooper's money, it had begun falling apart.

Mount Saint Helens is a volcano in Washington. It's near where Cooper likely landed.

This was an exciting clue. But no more clues were found. Many years went by.

FAST FACT

Mount Saint Helens **erupted** in May 1980. This event may have destroyed more clues.

Cooper jumped from the plane on a cold night during bad weather. He may have died after landing.

In 2016, the FBI stopped the investigation. Most experts believe Cooper did not survive. But his identity is still unknown.

ONE-MAN JOB?

It is unlikely that Cooper had help. He did not know the plane's flight path. So, he didn't know where he would land. He couldn't tell people on the ground where to meet him.

COMPREHENSION QUESTIONS

Write your answers on a separate piece of paper.

1. Write a few sentences describing what D. B. Cooper did.

2. Would you ever want to parachute from an airplane? Why or why not?

3. Where did D. B. Cooper's flight take off from?

    A. Seattle, Washington

    B. Portland, Oregon

    C. Mexico City

4. Why was finding Cooper's money a clue that he didn't survive?

    A. Cooper didn't want any money.

    B. Cooper said he'd give the money away.

    C. Cooper would have kept the money if he had lived.

5. What does *model* mean in this book?

Cooper jumped with two parachutes. One was a training model. It was sewn shut.

 A. a person in a fashion show
 B. an object used only for practice
 C. an object that works better than usual

6. What does *identity* mean in this book?

Most experts believe Cooper did not survive. But his identity is still unknown.

 A. who someone is
 B. what someone did
 C. what something costs

Answer key on page 32.

GLOSSARY

DNA
A chemical in the body that is unique to each person.

erupted
Sent hot gases, ash, and lava into the air.

evidence
Clues that can be used to help solve crimes.

FBI agents
People who work for a part of the US government that helps solve and stop crimes.

hijacker
A person who takes control of an airplane or other vehicle.

investigation
Work to find out the truth about something.

parachutes
Fabric that opens to slow people as they fall through the air.

skydiving
The sport of jumping from airplanes with parachutes.

suspects
People who the police think may be guilty of a crime.

TO LEARN MORE

BOOKS

Kim, Carol. *Disappearance of Skyjacker D. B. Cooper.* North Mankato, MN: Capstone Press, 2022.

Streissguth, Tom. *Investigating the D. B. Cooper Hijacking.* New York: AV2 by Weigl, 2020.

Sullivan, Tom. *Escape at 10,000 Feet: D. B. Cooper and the Missing Money.* New York: Balzer + Bray, 2021.

ONLINE RESOURCES

Visit www.apexeditions.com to find links and resources related to this title.

ABOUT THE AUTHOR

Arnold Ringstad lives in Minnesota with his wife and their cat. He enjoys researching and writing about mysterious events, such as the disappearance of D. B. Cooper.

INDEX

ANSWER KEY:
1. Answers will vary; 2. Answers will vary; 3. B; 4. C; 5. B; 6. A